# Just Joking 6

**NATIONAL GEOGRAPHIC KiDS**

**300** hilarious jokes about everything, including tongue twisters, riddles, and more!

Rosie Gowsell Pattison

NATIONAL GEOGRAPHIC
WASHINGTON, D.C.

Dinner's ready! Hyenas make a sound similar to a giggle. This sound tells other hyenas that they have food to share.

**KNOCK, KNOCK.**

*Who's there?*
Says.
*Says who?*
Says me, that's who!

Most geckos don't have eyelids. Instead they have clear membranes that they lick to keep clean.

6

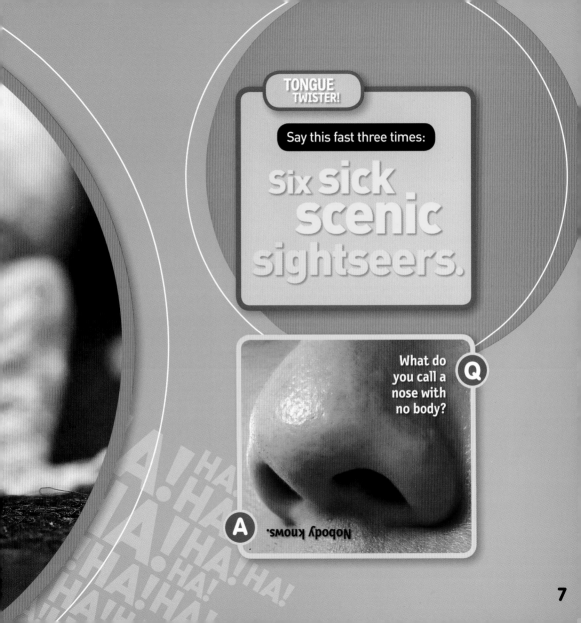

Say this fast three times:

# Six sick scenic sightseers.

What do you call a nose with no body?

Q

A

Nobody knows.

7

TONGUE TWISTER!

Say this fast three times:

Kristen's sister's biscuit mixer.

**Q** Where do pirates shop?

**A** At the maarrket.

**Q** What do you call an alligator eating Mexican food?

**A** A Taco-dile.

**Q** Which **superhero** works at a **dry cleaner** in his spare time?

**A** Iron Man.

8

Baby beluga whales are called calves. They are born gray or brown and turn white around five years old.

KNOCK, KNOCK.

Who's there?
Gnomie.
Gnomie who?
Don't you Gnomie?

KNOCK,
KNOCK.

*Who's there?*
Armageddon.
*Armageddon who?*
Armageddon out of here,
it's starting to rain!

Lions are very social animals.
They live in groups, called
prides, of 15 or more.

**Q** What kind of bird recycles?

**A** A two-can.

**Q** What do you get if you cross an ape and a prawn?

**A** A shrimpanzee.

12

Polar bears can weigh up to 1,200 pounds (544 kg) and can reach heights of 10 feet (3 m) tall when standing on their hind legs!

KNOCK, KNOCK.

*Who's there?*
Meow.
*Meow who?*
Open up this door right meow!

13

# What do snowmen eat for breakfast?

Snowflakes.

**TONGUE TWISTER!**

Say this fast three times:

**Sneaker speakers.**

**Q** What do you call a frog with no legs?

**A** Unhappy.

**Q** What do you get if you cross a slice of bread and a bloodsucking bug?

**A** Mosqui-toast.

**Q** What was the **fastest dinosaur?**

**A** A prontosaurus.

15

TONGUE
TWISTER!

Say this fast three times:

# Bamboo baboon.

17

The name "orangutan" means "person of the forest."

KNOCK, KNOCK.

*Who's there?*
Nana.
*Nana who?*
Nana your business!

18

**Q** Why did the **policeman** give the **gardener** a ticket?

**A** For disturbing the peas.

TONGUE TWISTER!

Say this fast three times:

**Extinct insects.**

19

**Q** How did the cheddar cheese feel after its vacation?

**A** It felt grate!

**Q** What kind of **lunch** do you get in the **desert?**

**A** Sand-wiches.

**Q** What do you call a sneezing train?

**A** Ah-choo-choo.

**Q** How did the rabbit do in her first show on Broadway?

**A** She gave a hare-raising performance.

KNOCK, KNOCK.

Who's there?
Havana.
Havana who?
We're Havana good time!

Some types of grouper fish are born as females and turn into males as they get older!

KNOCK,
KNOCK.

Who's there?
Acid.
Acid who?
Acid open
the door!

The arctic fox's feet
are covered in fur to
protect them from ice
and snow. It can endure
temperatures as low as
minus 58°F (-50°C).

Siamese cats are quite intelligent! They can be trained to fetch, retrieve, and even do tricks.

**KNOCK, KNOCK.**

*Who's there?*
Manatee.
*Manatee who?*
Manatee would be nice, I'm thirsty.

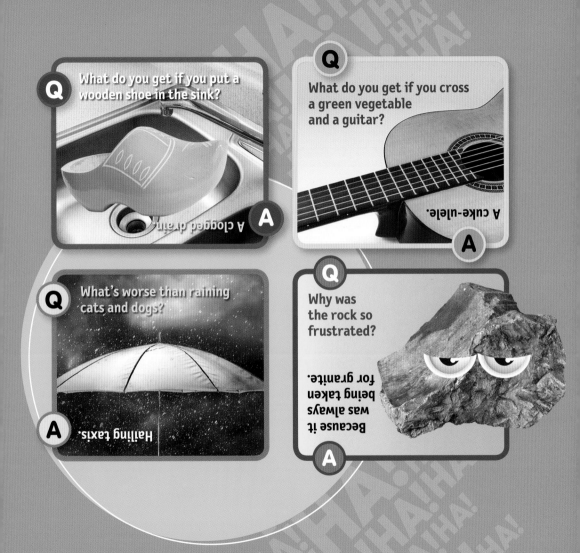

**Q** What do you get if you put a wooden shoe in the sink?

**A** A clogged drain.

**Q** What do you get if you cross a green vegetable and a guitar?

**A** A cuke-ulele.

**Q** What's worse than raining cats and dogs?

**A** Hailing taxis.

**Q** Why was the rock so frustrated?

**A** Because it was always being taken for granite.

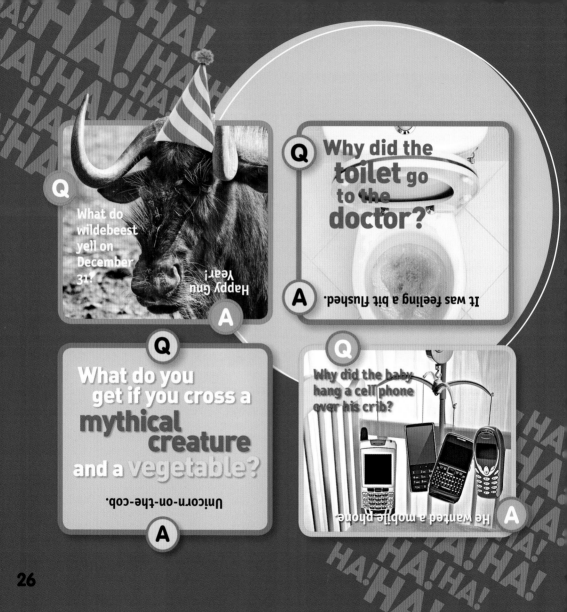

**Q** What do wildebeest yell on December 31?

**A** Happy Gnu Year!

**Q** Why did the **toilet** go to the **doctor?**

**A** It was feeling a bit flushed.

**Q** What do you get if you cross a **mythical creature** and a **vegetable?**

**A** Unicorn-on-the-cob.

**Q** Why did the baby hang a cell phone over his crib?

**A** He wanted a mobile phone.

Giant Galápagos turtles can survive for up to a year without eating or drinking.

**KNOCK, KNOCK.**

*Who's there?*
Wanda.
*Wanda who?*
Wanda hear another joke?

# Why was the dog sad when he returned home?

He had a ruff day.

KNOCK, KNOCK.

Who's there?
Yeast.
Yeast who?
You could at yeast open the door and say hello!

**Q** What do you call a **potato** that joins a **monastery?**

**A** A chip monk.

**Q** Why did the man marry a barbecue?

**A** Because it was the grill of his dreams.

**Q** What do you call a zombie in a Chinese restaurant kitchen?

**A** The Woking Dead.

**Q** What do you call it when you are scared by the same ghost twice?

**A** Deja-boo.

**Q** What does a janitor in an aquarium use to get the job done?

**A** All-porpoise cleaner.

**Q** What do you get if you cross an emperor and a vegetable?

**A** Genghis Corn.

32

Pelicans have air sacs in their bones to help them float on the water.

KNOCK, KNOCK.

Who's there?
Tibia.
Tibia who?
It's going tibia good day!

33

KNOCK,

KNOCK.

*Who's there?*
Nita.
*Nita who?*
Nita key to open
this door.

The red ruffed lemur gets
its name from the ruff of
fur around its neck.

**35**

What do you
get if you cross
an **elephant**
and a **ladybug?**

I don't know but you better hope it doesn't land on your arm!

FUNNY PUNS!

The giant boat sale was a big oar-deal!

**Q** What did the bees do after they moved into their new hive?

**A** They had a house-swarming party.

**Q** Why should you never lie to an x-ray technician?

**A** Because they can see right through you.

TONGUE TWISTER!

Say this fast three times:

**Stupid superstitions.**

**Q** Why is it fun to hang out with opera singers?

**A** Because they always leave you on a high note.

**Q** What is a crocodile's favorite party game?

**A** Swallow the leader.

HA! HA! HA! HA! HA! HA! HA! HA! HA!H

KNOCK, KNOCK.

*Who's there?*
Son.
*Son who?*
Son nice flowers in your garden!

Leftovers, anyone? A tiger will eat its kill until it is full and then hide it so it can return and continue eating when it is hungry again.

TONGUE TWISTER!

Say this fast three times:

# Five frantic frogs fled from fifty fierce fishes.

What do **pigs** write **letters** with?

By air mail
Par avion

to:
Mr. Kevin Bacon
Hollywood, California

Pig pens.

42

**Q** What kind of television shows do you watch in the kitchen?

**A** Soup operas.

CARRIE: Did you enjoy the tour of the cheese factory?

CHARLOTTE: A little bit cheesy, but I thought it was grate! Did you like it?

CARRIE: It could have been cheddar.

**Q** What kind of car does a chicken drive?

**A** A coop.

43

HA!HA!HA!HA!HA!HA!HA!HA!

**KNOCK,**

**KNOCK.**

*Who's there?*
Walnut.
*Walnut who?*
I walnut leave
without you.

Killer whales live in
groups called "pods."

44

**Q** What holiday do condiments celebrate?

**A** Cinco de mayo!

**Q** Why did the **orange** join the **navy?**

**A** Because it was a naval orange.

45

46

HA!HA!HA!
HA!HA!HA!HA!
HA!HA!HA!HA!
HA!HA!HA!HA!
HA!HA!HA!HA!
HA!HA!HA!
HA!HA!HA!

**Red foxes have excellent
nighttime vision and
do most of their hunting
at night.**

**Q** What is a
**sea monster's**
favorite dinner?

**A** Fish and ships.

**Q** Why did two coin collectors arrange a get-together?

**A** For old dimes' sake.

**Q** Why did the
**comedian**
stop at the
**fabric store?**

**A** He was looking for new material.

**FARMER 1: Who raided my vegetable patch?**

**FARMER 2: Beets me!**

# How does a seahorse get from one place to another quickly?

Seahorses use their tails to grasp objects and anchor themselves in one place.

It scallops.

There are around 200 different species of owls. A group of owls is called a parliament.

KNOCK, KNOCK.

Who's there?
Penny.
Penny who?
Penny for your thoughts?

**Q** Did you hear about the guy who had a **bungee jumping** accident?

**A** Don't worry, he is bouncing back.

**Q** What do you get if you cross a hairdresser and a laptop?

**A** A comb-puter.

**Q** What did one knife say to the other?

**A** Looking sharp!

**Q** How do astronauts serve dinner?

**A** In satellite dishes.

51

Don't be fooled by those short legs! Basset hounds have powerful noses and will give chase if they catch an interesting scent.

# Why did the dog bring a stick into the bank?

Because he was meeting the branch manager.

A baby great white shark is called a pup and can be up to 5 feet (1.5 m) long at birth.

KNOCK, KNOCK.

Who's there?
Whale.
Whale who?
I'm doing whale, how are you?

**Q**

What do you call it when someone steals your cup of coffee?

**A** A mugging.

**Q**

What starts with a T, ends with a T, and is full of T?

A teapot.

**A**

55

Why are guitars so nervous? **Q**

**A** Because they are high strung.

Say this fast three times:

**Rough rafting rapids.**

**Q** What has to be broken before you can use it?

**A** An egg.

What do you call a pig that can write with both hooves? **Q**

**A** Ham-bidextrous.

56

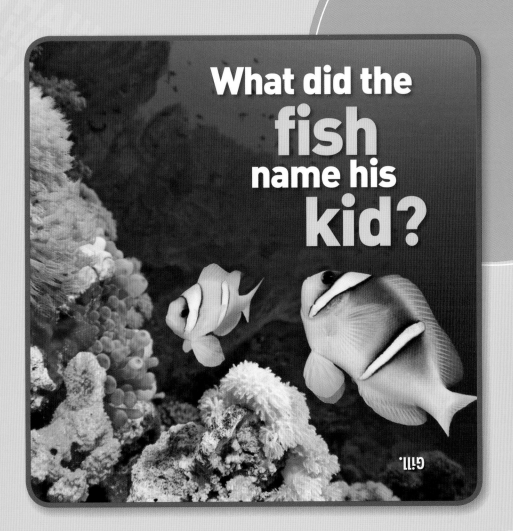

**What did the fish name his kid?**

Gill.

57

58

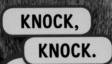

Draft horses are known for their tall stature and extremely muscular build. They can weigh up to 2,000 pounds (907 kg)!

**KNOCK, KNOCK.**

*Who's there?*
Feline.
*Feline who?*
I'm feline a little cold, can I come in?

**59**

Wake up! A lion may sleep up to 20 hours a day.

KNOCK, KNOCK.

Who's there?
Thumping.
Thumping who?
Thumping green and thlimy is crawling up your leg!

60

IRON 1: I need to speak with you immediately!

IRON 2: Is it a pressing matter?

**Q**

**What has one horn and gives milk?**

**A** A milk truck.

TONGUE TWISTER!

Say this fast three times:

**Mrs. Smith's fish sauce shop.**

**Q** Why did the gardener buy a new Weedwacker?

**A** Because he wanted cutting-hedge technology.

61

**Q** Why shouldn't you play basketball with a pig?

**A** Because they hog the ball.

TONGUE TWISTER!

Say this fast three times:

# There was a minimum of cinnamon.

It is believed that the female *T. rex* outweighed the male *T. rex* by a few thousand pounds.

KNOCK,

KNOCK.

*Who's there?*
Water.
*Water who?*
Water you doing?
Can you come out
and play?

64

# What do you call a sunbathing grizzly?

A solar bear.

65

KNOCK, KNOCK.

*Who's there?*
Ogre.
*Ogre who?*
Thought I'd come ogre for a visit.

66

Say this fast three times:

# Great Greek grape growers.

**Q**

Why are towels good comedians?

Because they have a dry sense of humor.

**A**

**Q**

What do you get if you cross **Bambi** and a **ghost?**

**A**

Bamboo.

CHEF:
How did you enjoy the soup?

DINER:
It was stew-pendous!

**Q**

How does Darth Vader like his toast?

**A**

On the dark side.

**Q**

Did the beluga have a good time at his birthday party?

**A**

He had a whale of a time!

68

Say this fast three times:

# Mr. Meminger's editor's sweater.

Raccoons have long, delicate fingers and a highly sensitive sense of touch.

KNOCK,

KNOCK.

Who's there?
Watson.
Watson who?
Watson TV tonight?

**INTERVIEWER:**
What is your favorite letter of the alphabet?

**PIRATE:**
You may think it's arrrr, but my first love be the c.

**Q** What is Tarzan's favorite Christmas song?

**A** Jungle Bells.

**Q** What does Godzilla call a motorcycle rider?

**A** Meals on wheels.

**KNOCK, KNOCK.**

Who's there?
Dozen.
Dozen who?
Dozen anyone want to let me in?

Bulldogs are one of the most popular mascots for universities and sports teams in the United States.

**73**

**Q** What do cattle wear when they join the army?

**A** Cowmooflage.

**Q** What do you get if you cross **detergent** and a **talk show host?**

**A** Soaprah Winfrey.

TONGUE TWISTER!

Say this fast three times:

Sheep should sleep in a shed.

**Q** Why did the shoe join a dating service?

**A** He was looking for his sole mate.

**What do dogs order in restaurants?**

Paw-sta.

Say this fast three times:

# Llamas lying lazily aloft a little log.

Dolphins have excellent hearing. Sounds travel through their lower jaws and into their inner ears.

KNOCK, KNOCK.

*Who's there?*
Walrus.
*Walrus who?*
Why do you walrus ask who's there?

**Q** What did one pumpkin say to the other pumpkin?

**A** Hey there gourd-geous!

TONGUE TWISTER!

Say this fast three times:

# Bob brought the black boot back.

79

**Q** What do you get if you cross a rock star with a horse?

**A** Jon Bon Pony.

TONGUE TWISTER!

Say this fast three times:

**Blue glue gun green glue gun**

I really wanted a **camouflage shirt** but I couldn't **find one.**

**Q** What do you get if you cross a pig and a president?

**A** Abra-ham Lincoln.

Baby robins are born with their eyes shut. They open around five days after hatching.

KNOCK, KNOCK.

Who's there?
Henrietta.
Henrietta who?
Henrietta whole pizza and has a stomachache.

81

Catfish have whiskers called barbels. They use them to find food and feel their way around.

KNOCK, KNOCK.

Who's there?
Adam.
Adam who?
Up and Adam, it's time to go!

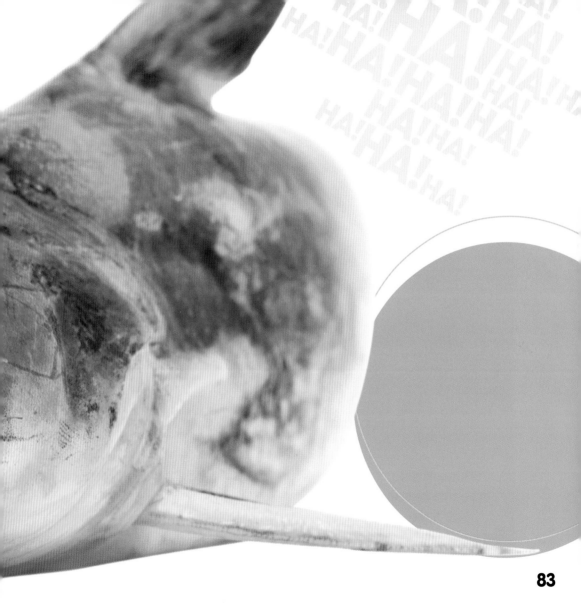

**83**

KNOCK, KNOCK.

*Who's there?*
Bacon.
*Bacon who?*
Whew, it's so hot I'm bacon out here!

Gray wolves are the largest members of the dog family. They can weigh up to 135 pounds (60 kg).

**Q** Who eats at underwater restaurants?

**A** Scuba diners.

**Q** How does music say goodbye?

**A** Audios.

**Q** What happens if you hire a kitten to work in a Mexican restaurant?

**A** You get guaco-meowly on your furrito.

**Q** What is a ghost's favorite holiday?

**A** April Ghouls' Day.

85

**Q**

How many boring people does it take to screw in a lightbulb?

**A** One.

**TONGUE TWISTER!**

Say this fast three times:

**Mad bunny, bad money.**

KNOCK, KNOCK.

Who's there?
Alden.
Alden who?
When you're Alden with your homework, come out and play!

TONGUE
TWISTER!

88

Say this fast three times:

Flapjack Jack flipped flat flapjacks.

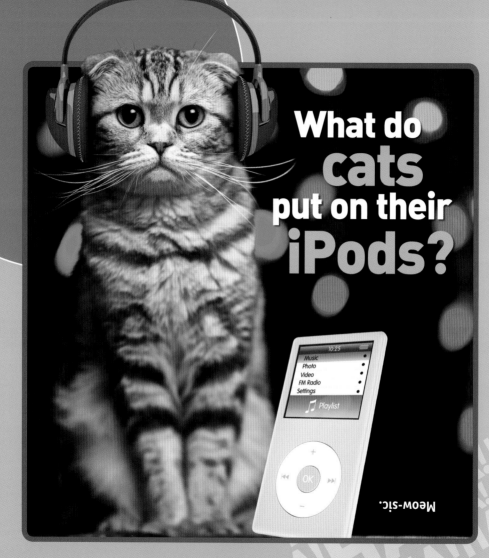

What do **cats** put on their **iPods?**

Meow-sic.

**Q** What do you call a skeleton that won't do his chores?

**A** Lazy bones.

**Q** What kind of snacks does a computer eat?

**A** Microchips.

**Q** What do you call a loaf of bread acting silly?

**A** A weirdough.

TONGUE TWISTER!

Say this fast three times:

**Santa's short suit shrunk.**

91

It was a terrible summer for Humpty Dumpty, but he had a great fall.

**Q**

What do you get if you cross an evergreen and a professor?

A tree-cher.

**A**

**Q**

What kind of street does a ghost live on?

A dead end.

**A**

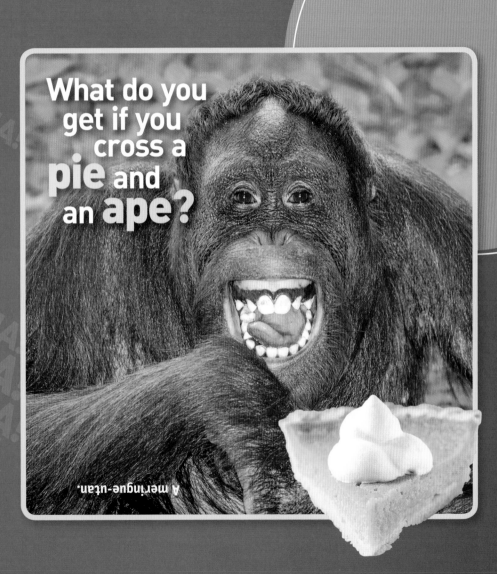

What do you get if you cross a **pie** and an **ape?**

A meringue-utan.

93

KNOCK, KNOCK.

Who's there?
Sonia.
Sonia who?
Sonia pizza guy making a delivery.

The closest relatives to hippos are cetaceans such as whales and dolphins.

# Why do no two female sheep look alike?

Because each one is ewe-nique.

HELLO
my name is
BAABAARA

HELLO
my name is

DOLLY

97

KNOCK, KNOCK.

Who's there?
Jamaican.
Jamaican who?
Jamaican dinner?
I'm starving.

Sloth bears feed on termites, honeybees, and fruit.

**Q** Why did the baker stop making donuts?

**A** She got tired of the hole thing.

Say this fast three times:

Ghost hosts boast the most.

**Q** What is a ghost's favorite meal?

**A** Gum-boo.

**TONGUE TWISTER!**

Say this fast three times:

Swim, swam, swum.

**Q** What do you get if you cross a pig and a cactus?

**A** A porker-pine.

**Q** Why are **writers** so **logical?**

**A** Because they have a lot of comma sense.

100

A zebra's stripe pattern is as unique as a human's fingerprint.

KNOCK, KNOCK.

Who's there?
Eddie.
Eddie who?
Eddie body want to hear a knock-knock joke?

# What do get if you cross a *T. rex* and a lemon?

A dino-sour.

103

After a cheetah chases down its dinner, it needs half an hour to catch its breath before eating.

**KNOCK, KNOCK.**

*Who's there?*
Kent.
*Kent who?*
Kent you tell by the sound of my voice?

**Q** Why did the tiny pepper put on a sweater?

**A** He was a little chili.

**Q** What sport does Bigfoot like to play?

**A** Sas-squash.

Say this fast three times:

**Crisp crusts crackle crunchily.**

**Q** What do you call a shark giving presents?

**A** Santa Jaws.

**Q** What do you get if you cross a cow and an octopus?

**A** A cow that can milk itself.

**Q** What kind of bugs live in an apartment?

**A** Ten-ants.

**Q** What has a **neck but no head?**

**A** A bottle.

**Q** What do vegetarian zombies eat?

**A** Graaaaaaains!

# Which barnyard animal can sing and dance?

Justin Timberlamb.

KNOCK,
KNOCK.

Who's there?
Isadore.
Isadore who?
Isadore locked?

Only the males are called peacocks. The females are called peahens!

What kind of car does an insect drive? **Q**

A Volkswagen Beetle. **A**

TONGUE TWISTER!

Say this fast three times:

# Turbo sherbet.

KNOCK, KNOCK.

*Who's there?*
Butternut.
*Butternut who?*
Butternut be late
for the movie.

110

American alligators have upward-facing nostrils that let them breathe while the rest of their body is underwater.

**Q** What do you get if you cross two snakes and a car window?

**A** Windshield vipers.

**Q** What kind of band do killer whales play in?

**A** An orca-stra.

HA!HA!HA!HA!HA!HA!HA!HA!

112

I spy with my little eye ...
The lynx has excellent vision.
It can spot prey from 250 feet
(75 m) away.

KNOCK,
KNOCK.

Who's there?
A herd.
A herd who?
A herd you were lonely
so I came to visit.

113

# What do you get if you cross a shaggy dog and a couch?

Fur-niture.

KNOCK, KNOCK.

Who's there?
Zombies.
Zombies who?
BRAINS!!!!!

Seals can stay underwater for up to 15 minutes.

116

Say this fast three times:

# Imaginary menagerie.

**Q** What gets wet while it is drying?

A towel. **A**

117

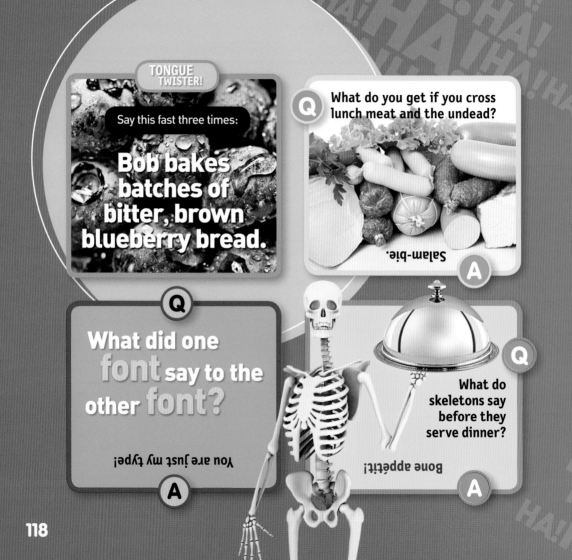

TONGUE TWISTER!

Say this fast three times:

**Bob bakes batches of bitter, brown blueberry bread.**

**Q** What do you get if you cross lunch meat and the undead?

**A** Salam-bie.

**Q** What did one font say to the other font?

**A** You are just my type!

**Q** What do skeletons say before they serve dinner?

**A** Bone appétit!

118

# Where do **fish** post their **photographs?**

On Fin-stagram.

Gorillas are very intelligent. Some have even learned sign language!

HA! HA! HA! HA! HA! HA! HA! HA! HA! HA! HA! HA!

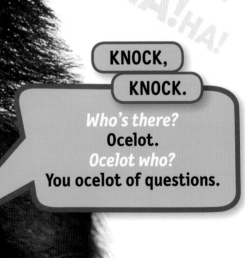

KNOCK, KNOCK.

*Who's there?*
Ocelot.
*Ocelot who?*
You ocelot of questions.

121

When an elephant is thirsty, it can suck around 2 gallons (7.5 L) of water into its trunk to spray down its throat to drink.

KNOCK, KNOCK.

Who's there?
House.
House who?
House about we go for a walk?

**Q** What do pirates say on Halloween?

**A** Trick arrrr treat!

LISA: Hey! Someone stole my recliner!

FRED: I couldn't chair less.

**Q** What do you get if you cross a **superhero** and a box of **cereal**?

**A** Iron Bran.

**Q** What is a hog's favorite type of cookie?

**A** Pig Newtons.

**Q** What do you call a vampire that eats too many beans?

**A** Count Flatula.

**Q** How many oranges grow on a tree?

**A** All of them.

TONGUE TWISTER!

Say this fast three times:

**Mimicking my hiccupping.**

124

# What do dogs like to eat for breakfast?

Barkon and wooffles.

125

# Why do polar bears have fur coats?

Because they would look silly in sweaters.

A horse's eyes are on the sides of its head. Horses can see almost 360 degrees around themselves!

KNOCK, KNOCK.

Who's there?
Annie.
Annie who?
Annie one going to open the door?

**What kind of animal works at the bank?**

Q

A loan wolf.

A

TONGUE TWISTER!

Say this fast three times:

**Cheap ship trip.**

129

**SPIDER 1:**
Hey, do you like my new web?

**SPIDER 2:**
It's unbe-weave-able!

**Q** What football position do dogs play?

**A** Wide retriever.

**Q** What's the best side of the house to build a porch on?

**A** The outside.

130

Bald eagles have been the national symbol of the United States since 1782.

KNOCK, KNOCK.

Who's there?
Carmen.
Carmen who?
Carmen see for yourself!

131

Look out! A skunk can
spray its scent up to 12
feet (3.7 m) away!

KNOCK,
KNOCK.

Who's there?
Randy.
Randy who?
Randy marathon and
boy am I tired!

Say this fast three times:

# Chester chews a chunk of cheap cheddar cheese.

Q How do prisoners phone each other?

A On their cell phones.

Q Did you hear about the new Mexican restaurant?

A It's the taco the town.

Q What kind of car does a baker drive?

A A hy-bread.

Q What kind of band plays snappy music?

A A rubber band.

135

TONGUE TWISTER!

Say this fast three times:

Real rural walrus.

Q What kind of medicine do you give a sick bed?

A Pill-os.

HA! HA! HA! HA! HA! HA! HA! HA! HA! HA! HA! HA! HA! HA! HA!

# What do you call a surprised turtle?

Shell-shocked.

HONK! Canada geese call to each other with loud honks while flying.

KNOCK, KNOCK.

Who's there?
Gretta.
Gretta who?
Gretta move on, we are going to be late!

**Q** Why did the chef go to jail?

**A** He was caught beating an egg.

**Q** What do you get if you cross a wizard and a horse?

**A** Harry Trotter.

**Q** Why did the hockey coach put a dog on the ice?

**A** They needed a rufferee.

**Q** Why don't chemists like to tell jokes?

**A** Because they don't get a reaction.

141

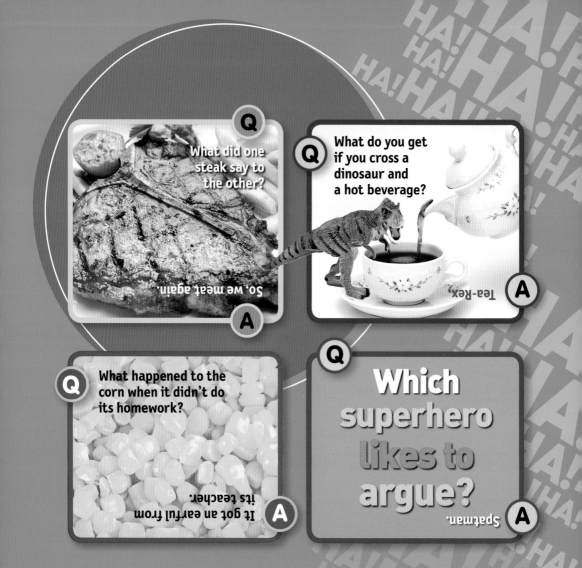

142

# What is an egg's favorite horror movie?

The Eggsorcist.

Puffer fish aren't very good swimmers. They suck up water and "puff up" like a balloon to protect themselves from predators they are too slow to swim away from.

**KNOCK, KNOCK.**

*Who's there?*
Luke.
*Luke who?*
**Luke through the peephole and find out!**

HA!HA!HA!
HA!HA! HA!
HA! HA!
HA!HA!
HA!

145

What kind of fruit has a bad attitude?

A grizzly pear.

148

Say this fast three times:

# Higgledy-piggledy.

What kind of watch does a witch wear? **Q**

**A** A Time-hex.

**Q** What kind of tests do chickens take?

**A** Egg-sams.

**Q** What has **four wheels** and **flies?**

**A** A garbage truck.

TONGUE TWISTER!

Say this fast three times:

Eleven **excited elves** exchanged expensive **earrings.**

**Q** Why did the customer try to pay for his car with feathers?

**A** He heard he had to make a down payment.

**Why did the cowboy adopt a dachshund?**

To get a long little doggy!

Say this fast three times:

# Six sharp smart sharks.

153

KNOCK, KNOCK.

*Who's there?*
Ammonia.
*Ammonia who?*
Ammonia gonna knock
one more time, then
I'm leaving.

The spectacled langur
monkey is named for the
white circles around its
eyes that look like glasses.

**Q** What should you do with deviled eggs?

**A** Give them an eggs-orcism.

**Q** What shoes do ghosts wear when it's cold?

BOO!

**A** Booooots.

155

**Q** Why should you never lend your neighbor a rake?

**A** Because they will always come back for mower.

**Q** What did the jar of paste do on January 1?

**A** It made a Glue Year's resolution.

**Q** Which superhero works in an ice cream shop?

**A** Scooper-man.

**Q** What do you get if you cross a car and a famous Paris cathedral?

**A** The Hatchback of Notre Dame.

**KNOCK, KNOCK.**

*Who's there?*
Icy.
*Icy who?*
Icy a monster out here, open the door!

There are around 30 different types of terriers. They range in size from 2 to 70 pounds (1 to 32 kg).

Looks like trouble! A group of goldfish is called a troubling.

KNOCK, KNOCK.

Who's there?
Ozzie.
Ozzie who?
Ozzie you later, alligator!

159

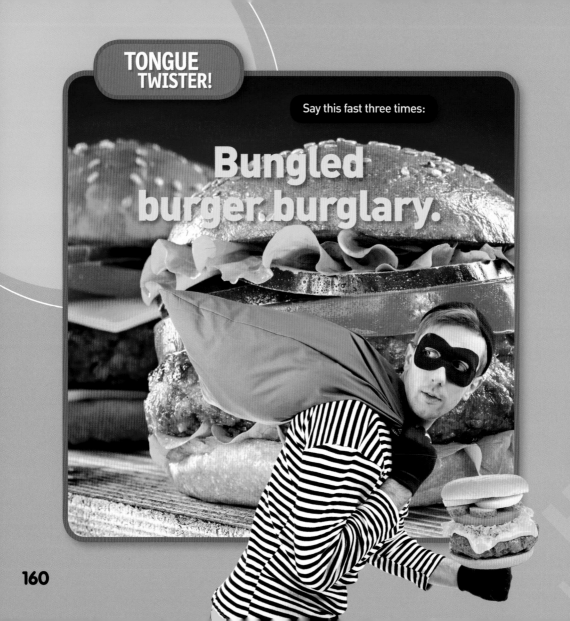

TONGUE TWISTER!

Say this fast three times:

# Bungled burger burglary.

160

**Q** What has two claws, four wheels, and a meter?

**A** A taxi crab.

**Q** What's the only coat you put on wet?

**A** A coat of paint.

**Q** What do you get if you cross a cow and a duck?

**A** Milk and quackers.

**Q** What kind of jokes do farmers like?

**A** Corny ones.

**Q** How does the car muffler feel when it gets home?

**A** Exhausted.

**Q** What do you call a horse that is starring in a play?

**A** The mane attraction.

KNOCK, KNOCK.

Who's there?
Genoa.
Genoa who?
Genoa good restaurant? I'm hungry.

Only adult male cardinals have the distinctive red plumage. Females and babies are brown or gray with hints of red.

TONGUE TWISTER!

Say this fast three times:

# Feathered finches flinch while flying forward fast.

164

Finches live on every continent in the world except Antarctica and Australia.

KNOCK,
KNOCK.
Who's there?
Ham.
*Ham who?*
Ham I going to
come in?

A monitor lizard can
dislocate a bone in its
throat so it can swallow
its food whole.

**TONGUE TWISTER!**

Say this fast three times:

**Six slim sycamore saplings.**

Q What do you get if you cross a lamb and Japanese food?

A Su-sheep.

167

**KNOCK, KNOCK.**

*Who's there?*
Sir Chadworth Huffington.
*Sir Chadworth Huffington who?*
Do you really know more than one Sir Chadworth Huffington?

The blue and green macaw can live up to 50 years.

169

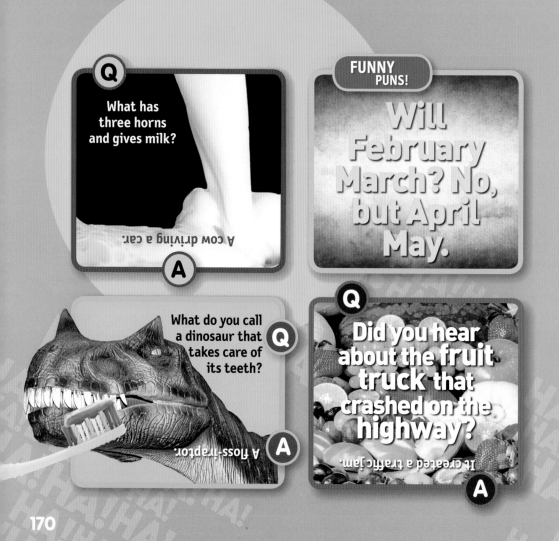

**Q**

What has three horns and gives milk?

**A** A cow driving a car.

Will February March? No, but April May.

What do you call a dinosaur that takes care of its teeth? **Q**

**A** A floss-iraptor.

**Q** Did you hear about the fruit truck that crashed on the highway?

It created a traffic jam. **A**

170

**TONGUE TWISTER!**

Say this fast three times:

# Sick salamanders sipped and slurped soup.

171

What do you call a nut with facial hair?

A mustachio.

172

**Q**

What do Dracula and a lollipop have in common?

**A** They are both suckers.

TONGUE TWISTER!

Say this fast three times:

**Hordes of Nords stormed the fjords.**

**Q**

What kind of truck does a pig drive?

**A** An 18-squealer.

**Q**

What did Darth Vader name his daughter?

**A** Ella Vader.

173

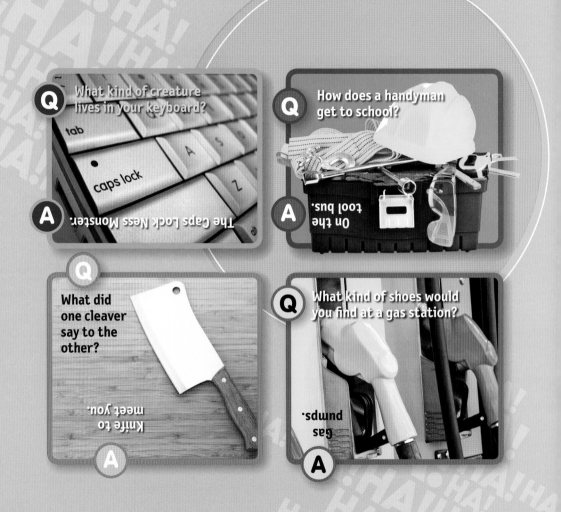

**Q** What kind of creature lives in your keyboard?

tab

caps lock

**A** The Caps Lock Ness Monster.

**Q** How does a handyman get to school?

**A** On the tool bus.

**Q** What did one cleaver say to the other?

Knife to meet you.

**A**

**Q** What kind of shoes would you find at a gas station?

Gas pumps.

**A**

174

Goats do not like to get wet and will seek shelter when it is raining.

KNOCK,

KNOCK.

Who's there?
Jewel.
Jewel who?
Jewel remember me when you see my face.

175

# Where do fish go on vacation?

Fin-land.

177

KNOCK,
KNOCK.

*Who's there?*
Harmony.
*Harmony who?*
Harmony more
knock-knock jokes
do you want to hear?

When hibernating, a bear's
heart rate can fall from
40 beats a minute to
8 beats a minute.

**Q** Why did the dog go to the bank?

**A** To make a de-paws-it.

**Q** What did one fish that was caught in a net say to the other?

**A** Well, this is a fine mesh you got us into!

**Q** Why shouldn't you play cards with a hard-boiled egg?

**A** It is hard to beat.

GIRL 1:
Want to go shopping with me?

GIRL 2:
Nah, seen one shopping center, you've seen a mall.

TONGUE TWISTER!

Say this fast three times:

**Thin sticks, thick bricks.**

**KNOCK, KNOCK.**

*Who's there?*
Ears.
*Ears who?*
Ears another joke for you.

Chimpanzees are more closely related to humans than to gorillas or orangutans.

KNOCK, KNOCK.

Who's there?
Kanga.
*Kanga who?*
No, it's called
a kangaROO.

Mummified remains of Chihuahuas have been found in Mesoamerican grave sites. It was believed that these little dogs helped the owners travel to the afterlife safely.

What do you get if you cross a **sad dog** and a **fruit salad?**

A melon collie.

184

**Q** What kind of clothing does a house wear?

**A** A-dress.

ELLEN: How do you like your soft drink?

JIM: It is soda-licious!

TONGUE TWISTER!

Say this fast three times:

**Shelley sells shades.**

**Q** Did you hear about the fire at the shoe factory?

**A** One hundred soles were lost.

185

**Q**

## What is 1,450 feet (440 m) tall and drinks blood?

**A**

The Vampire State Building.

**Q** What kind of cell phone do you buy at a fruit stand?

A Blackberry.

**A**

KNOCK, KNOCK.

Who's there?
Walter.
Walter who?
Walter you doing today?

Kookaburras make loud, long calls that sound like laughter.

TONGUE TWISTER!

188

# Double bubble gum trouble.

189

Hyenas live in large groups called clans. There can be up to 80 hyenas in a clan.

KNOCK, KNOCK.

Who's there?
Viper.
Viper who?
Viper feet, your shoes are wet.

**Q** Why is a frog always happy?

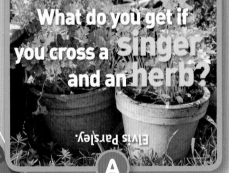

**A** It eats whatever bugs him.

**Q** How can you tell when a **wedding cake** is sad?

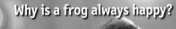

**A** It's in tiers.

**Q** What do you get if you cross a **singer** and an **herb?**

**A** Elvis Parsley.

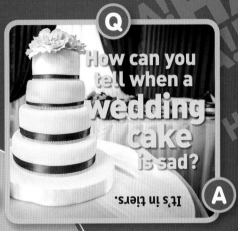

CROCODILE 1:
Did you have a good time at the comedy club?

CROCODILE 2:
I was croc-ing up laughing!

**Q** What kind of **monster** lives near your **stomach?**

**A** The abdominal snowman.

**Q** Where do you find a turtle with no legs?

**A** Right where you left it.

TONGUE TWISTER!

Say this fast three times:

**Thistle-sifter.**

**Q** What do you get if you cross a frog and an automobile?

**A** A car that can jump-start itself.

192

Penguins produce a waterproofing oil that they spread all over their bodies.

KNOCK, KNOCK.

Who's there?
Noah.
Noah who?
I Noah lot more jokes!

Sometimes dogs have two
different-colored eyes. This is
called heterochromia.

KNOCK, KNOCK.

Who's there?
Pencil.
Pencil who?
Your pencil fall down if you don't wear a belt.

A group of ring-tailed lemurs is called a troop.

KNOCK, KNOCK.

Who's there?
Radio.
Radio who?
Radio not, here I come!

196

SLUG 1: Hey, how do you think you did on our math test?

SLUG 2: I snailed it!

Say this fast three times:

# Miss Mix picks chicks.

Say this fast three times:

Sixish.
Sixish.
Sixish.

Q

What do witches use to style their hair?

A
Scare spray.

Q
What kind of ghost haunts a chicken coop?

A
A poultry-geist.

198

What is a **kitten's** favorite **day** of the **week?**

Cat-urday.

KNOCK, KNOCK.

Who's there?
Peas.
Peas who?
Peas tell me there are no more knock-knock jokes!

Giant pandas are one of the world's rarest animals. There are only about 1,000 living in the wild.

# JOKEFINDER

# ILLUSTRATIONCREDITS

102 (bottom), Africa Studio/SS; 103, Cuson/SS; 104, Maggy Meyer/SS; 105 (bottom, right), Kim Nguyen/SS; 105 (bottom, right), Elizabeth Hoffmann/SS; 105 (bottom, right), Kim Nguyen/SS; 105 (top, left), Ruslan Kudrin/SS; 105 (top, left), Maks Narodenko/SS; 106 (bottom, right), Aboikis/SS; 106 (bottom, right), Trenzy/SS; 106 (top, left), Channarong Meesuk/SS; 106 (top, left), Aa3/SS; 106 (top, right), Jessica Kirsh/SS; 107 (bottom, left), Montego/SS; 107 (right), Erik Lam/SS; 107 (right), Paket/SS; 107 (top, right), John Abbate/SS; 108, Nagel Photography/SS; 109 (bottom, right), Kentoh/SS; 109 (top, right), Andrey Pavlov/SS; 110, Robert Eastman/SS; 112 (bottom), Christopher Meder/SS; 112 (top), Christian Mueller/SS; 113, Michael Wick/SS; 114, Maria Kraynova/SS; 115, Eleana/SS; 116, Olga_gl/SS; 117 (bottom, right), Dzaky Murad/SS; 118 (bottom, right), RT Images/SS; 118 (bottom, right), Gen Epic Solutions/SS; 118 (top, right), R_Szatkowski/SS; 118 (top, right), Alexei Logvinovich/SS; 119, Motorolka/SS; 119 (bottom), Vasin Lee/SS; 120, Eric Isselee/DRMS; 122, Mark O'Flaherty/SS; 123 (left), Tovkach Oleg/SS; 123 (top, right), Dennis/SS; 124 (top, left), Panbazil/SS; 124 (top, right), Vetasster/SS; 124 (bottom, left), Anch/SS; 124 (bottom, left), Africa Studio/SS; 125 (bottom), Andrey_Kuzmin/SS; 125 (top), Annette Shaff/SS; 126, Cindy Creighton/SS; 128, Sari ONeal/SS; 129 (bottom, right), Jules Kitano/SS; 130 (left), Tetiana Yurchenko/SS; 130 (bottom, left), Karamysh/SS; 130 (top, right), WilleeCole Photography/SS; 131, Teri Virbickis/SS; 132, Eric Isselee/SS; 134, Southern Light Studios/SS; 135 (bottom, left), Diana Valujeva/SS; 135 (bottom, left), Val Lawless/SS; 135 (top, right), Bernd Juergens/SS; 136 (bottom, left), Atiketta Sangasaeng/SS; 136 (top, left), Aleksei Verhovski/SS; 137, Annette Shaff/SS; 138, Rusty Dodson/SS; 140, David P. Lewis/SS; 141 (bottom, left), zow/SS; 141 (bottom, right), Ralf Maassen (DTEurope)/SS; 141 (top, left), Africa Studio/SS; 141 (top, right), Chamille White/SS; 141 (top, right), Accept Photo/SS; 142 (bottom, left), Alexandra Lande/SS; 142 (top, left), Erwinova/SS; 142 (top, right), M. Unal Ozmen/SS; 142 (top, right), Andrea Ricordi/SS; 143, Boris Rabtsevich/SS; 143 (bottom, left), M. Unal Ozmen/SS; 143 (bottom, right), M. Unal Ozmen/SS; 144, Eric Isselee/SS; 146, Serg64/SS; 148, John Michael Evan Potter/SS; 149 (bottom, right), David Evison/SS; 149 (bottom, right), Nikuwka/SS; 149 (top, right), Evgeny Karandaev/SS; 150 (bottom, left), Shebeko/SS; 150 (bottom, right), Rustamir/SS; 150 (bottom, right), Rustamir/SS; 150 (top, left), Denis Nata/SS; 150 (top, left), Wikrom/SS; 151, Annette Shaff/SS; 152, Sergey Uryadnikov/SS; 152 (top), Juan Carlos Tinjaca/SS; 154, Palo_ok/SS; 155 (bottom, left), Debbie Vinci/SS; 155 (bottom, left), TerraceStudio/SS; 155 (bottom, right), Kucher Serhii/SS; 155 (bottom, right), Bonchan/SS; 156 (bottom, left), M. Unal Ozmen/SS; 156 (top, left), Africa Studio/SS; 156 (top, right), BW Folsom/SS; 157, Otsphoto/SS; 158 (bottom, left), ANP/SS; 158 (right), Vangert/SS; 160 (bottom, right), Africa Studio/SS; 160 (bottom, right), Indigolotos/SS; 160 (top), Primopiano/SS; 161 (bottom, left), Denis Nata/SS; 161 (bottom, left), Smereka/SS; 161 (bottom, right), John Kasawa/SS; 161 (top, left), Nykonchuk Oleksii/SS; 161 (top, right), Veerachai Viteeman/SS; 162 (bottom, left), Eric Isselee/SS; 162 (bottom, left), Repina Valeriya/SS; 162 (top, left), Freer/SS; 163, Charles Brutlag/DRMS; 164, Steven Russel lSmith Photos/SS; 166, Sprocky/SS; 167 (bottom, right), Phongsak Chartphet/SS; 167 (bottom, right), Marcelo_Krelling/SS; 167 (top, right), Jo Crebbin/SS; 168, Eric Isselee/SS; 170 (bottom, left), Willequet Manuel/SS; 170 (bottom, left), Macbrianmun/SS; 170 (bottom, right), Supot Suebwongsa/SS; 170 (top, left), Schankz/SS; 170 (top, right), David M. Schrader/SS; 171, Kazakov Maksim/SS; 171, Julia Sudnitskaya/SS; 172, Twonix Studio/SS; 172, Graletta/SS; 173 (bottom, left), Antpkr/SS; 173 (top, left), Svetlana Foote/SS; 173 (top, left), Paul Michael Hughes/SS; 173 (top, right), Strahil Dimitrov/SS; 174 (top, left), Jason Nemeth/SS; 174 (top, right), Africa Studio/SS; 174 (bottom, left), Africa Studio/SS; 174 (bottom, right), Apples Eyes Studio/SS; 175, Imageman/SS; 176, LauraD/SS; 176 (bottom), Africa Studio/SS; 177, BW Folsom/SS; 178, Pavel Kovacs/SS; 179 (top, right), Bullet74/SS; 179 (bottom, right), Puwanai/SS; 180 (bottom, right), Peter Gudella/SS; 180 (top, right), Africa Studio/SS; 180 (bottom, left), Dancestrokes/SS; 180 (top, left), Diana Valujeva/SS; 181, Pavel Kovacs/SS; 182, Andrey Kuzmin/DRMS; 184, Twilight Artistry/SS; 184 (bottom, left), Margouillat Photo/SS; 185 (top, left), Joel_420/SS; 185 (bottom, left), Hobbit/SS; 185 (top, right), Mahathir Mohd Yasin/SS; 185 (bottom, right), Anteromite/SS; 186 (bottom, left), Ad Stock RF/SS; 186 (bottom, left), Kryvenok Anastasiia/SS; 187, Shadow Mac/SS; 188, Marie C Fields/SS; 190, Bonga 1965/SS; 191 (top, left), Gaschwald/SS; 191 (bottom, left), Floydine/SS; 191 (bottom, right), Dave Montreuil/SS; 191 (top, right), Robert-Horvat/SS; 191 (bottom, left), Paco Toscano/SS; 191 (top, right), Jsbdueck/SS; 191 (bottom, right), Eric Isselee/SS; 191 (bottom, right), Nagy-Bagoly Arpad/SS; 193, Volodymyr Goinyk/SS; 194, Patryk Kosmider/SS; 196, Tao Jiang/SS; 197 (top, right), Lisa S./SS; 197 (top, right), QiuJu Song/SS; 197 (bottom, right), Volodymyr Burdiak/SS; 198 (bottom, left), Steve Collender/SS; 198 (bottom, right), Aksenova Natalya/SS; 198 (top, right), Oksana2010/SS; 199, Marlinde/SS; 200, Hung Chung Chih/SS;

**207**

**Published by the National Geographic Society**

Gary E. Knell, *President and Chief Executive Officer*
John M. Fahey, *Chairman of the Board*
Declan Moore, *Executive Vice President; President, Publishing and Travel*
Melina Gerosa Bellows, *Publisher and Chief Creative Officer,*
  *Books, Kids, and Family*

**Prepared by the Book Division**

Hector Sierra, *Senior Vice President and General Manager*
Nancy Laties Feresten, *Senior Vice President, Kids Publishing and Media*
Jennifer Emmett, *Vice President, Editorial Director, Kids Books*
Eva Absher-Schantz, *Design Director, Kids Publishing and Media*
Jay Sumner, *Director of Photography, Kids Publishing*
R. Gary Colbert, *Production Director*
Jennifer A. Thornton, *Director of Managing Editorial*

**Staff for This Book**

Shelby Alinsky, *Project Editor*
Julide Dengel, *Art Director*
Lisa Jewell, *Photo Editor*
Paige Towler, *Editorial Assistant*
Callie Broaddus, *Design Production Assistant*
Margaret Leist, *Photo Assistant*
Grace Hill, *Associate Managing Editor*
Mike O'Connor, *Production Editor*
Lewis R. Bassford, *Production Manager*
Susan Borke, *Legal and Business Affairs*

**Production Services**

Phillip L. Schlosser, *Senior Vice President*
Chris Brown, *Vice President, NG Book Manufacturing*
George Bounelis, *Senior Production Manager*
Nicole Elliott, *Director of Production*
Rachel Faulise, *Manager*
Robert L. Barr, *Manager*

**Editorial, Design, and Production by Plan B Book Packagers**

For more information, please visit nationalgeographic.com,
call 1-800-NGS LINE (647-5463), or write to the following address:
National Geographic Society
1145 17th Street N.W.
Washington, D.C. 20036-4688 U.S.A.

Visit us online at nationalgeographic.com/books

For librarians and teachers: ngchildrensbooks.org

More for kids from National Geographic: kids.nationalgeographic.com

For information about special discounts for bulk purchases, please contact National Geographic Books Special Sales: ngspecsales@ngs.org

For rights or permissions inquiries, please contact National Geographic Books Subsidiary Rights: ngbookrights@ngs.org

Paperback ISBN: 978-1-4263-1735-4
Reinforced Library Binding ISBN: 978-1-4263-1736-1

Printed in China

14/PPS/1